# MORTGAGE MASTERY: THE ULTIMATE GUIDE TO SAVING MONEY ON YOUR HOME MORTGAGE

## 1.    Introduction

**Importance of saving money when applying for a home mortgage**

Saving money when applying for a home mortgage is crucial for several reasons:

1. Lower Down Payment: Saving money allows you to make a larger down payment on your mortgage. A higher down payment reduces the amount you need to borrow, which can result in a lower loan amount and lower monthly mortgage payments. It can also help you avoid private mortgage insurance (PMI) if you can put down at least 20% of the home's purchase price.

2. Reduced Interest Payments: By saving money and making a larger down payment, you can potentially secure a lower interest rate on your mortgage. A lower interest rate can save you thousands of dollars over the life of your loan. Additionally, having a larger down payment can help you qualify for more favorable loan terms, such as a shorter loan term or a lower interest rate.

3. Improved Debt-to-Income Ratio: Lenders consider your debt-to-income ratio when approving your mortgage application. By saving money and reducing your debt burden, you can lower your debt-to-income ratio, making you a more attractive borrower to lenders. This can increase your chances of mortgage approval and potentially qualify you for better loan terms.

4. Enhanced Financial Stability: Saving money for a home mortgage demonstrates financial responsibility and stability to lenders. It shows that you are capable of managing your finances and have the means to handle mortgage payments. Lenders are more likely to offer favorable loan terms to borrowers who have demonstrated the ability to save money and responsibly manage their finances.

5. Emergency Fund: Saving money for a home mortgage allows you to build an emergency fund. Having an emergency fund provides a safety net in case of unexpected expenses or financial hardships. It can help you avoid defaulting on your mortgage payments and protect your investment in your home.

6. Flexibility and Peace of Mind: Saving money before applying for a home mortgage gives you flexibility and peace of mind. It allows you to have funds available for closing costs, moving expenses, and any necessary repairs or renovations. Having savings also provides a cushion for unexpected changes in your financial situation, such as job loss or medical emergencies.

In summary, saving money when applying for a home mortgage is important because it can lower your down payment, reduce interest payments, improve your debt-to-income ratio, enhance financial stability, provide an emergency fund, and offer flexibility and peace of mind. It allows you to secure better loan terms, save money over the life of your mortgage, and protect yourself from financial uncertainties.

**Overview of the book's content and benefits**

"Mortgage Mastery: The Ultimate Guide to Saving Money on Your Home Mortgage" is a comprehensive book that aims to provide readers with the knowledge and strategies to effectively manage their home mortgage and save money in the process. Here is an overview of the book's content and benefits:

1. Understanding Mortgages: The book starts by explaining the basics of mortgages, including the different types of mortgages available, interest rates, and terms. It helps readers gain a clear

understanding of how mortgages work, empowering them to make informed decisions.

2. Mortgage Planning: The book delves into the importance of mortgage planning and offers valuable insights on how to choose the right mortgage for your financial situation. It covers topics such as budgeting, credit scores, and loan pre-approval, helping readers navigate the mortgage process with confidence.

3. Negotiating Mortgage Terms: This section of the book focuses on teaching readers how to negotiate favorable mortgage terms with lenders. It provides practical tips and techniques to secure lower interest rates, reduce closing costs, and negotiate other favorable terms that can result in significant savings over the life of the mortgage.

4. Refinancing and Loan Modification: "Mortgage Mastery" also explores the benefits and considerations of refinancing and loan modification. It explains when and how to refinance a mortgage to take advantage of lower interest rates or to change the loan terms to better suit your financial goals. It also covers loan modification options for those facing financial difficulties.

5. Strategies to Save Money: The book offers a range of strategies and techniques to help readers save money on their home mortgage. It includes advice on making extra payments, bi-weekly payment plans, and strategies to shorten the loan term, all of which can result in substantial interest savings.

6. Avoiding Common Mortgage Mistakes: "Mortgage Mastery" provides guidance on common mistakes to avoid during the mortgage process. It educates readers about potential pitfalls and how to steer clear of them, ensuring a smoother and more cost-effective mortgage experience.

The benefits of reading "Mortgage Mastery: The Ultimate Guide to Saving Money on Your Home Mortgage" include:

- Empowerment: The book equips readers with the knowledge and tools to make informed decisions about their home mortgage, empowering them to take control of their financial future.

- Savings: By implementing the strategies and techniques outlined in the book, readers can potentially save a significant amount of money over the life of their mortgage.

- Confidence: Understanding the mortgage process and being aware of potential pitfalls builds confidence in navigating the complex world of mortgages.

- Financial Security: By optimizing their mortgage, readers can free up funds for other financial goals, such as saving for retirement or paying off other debts.

Overall, "Mortgage Mastery" serves as a comprehensive guide for anyone looking to save money on their home mortgage. It offers practical advice, valuable insights, and actionable strategies to help readers make the most of their mortgage and achieve long-term financial success.

## 2.      Understanding the Mortgage Process

**Explanation of the mortgage process**

The mortgage process refers to the steps involved in obtaining a home loan. Here is an explanation of the mortgage process:

1. Prequalification: The first step is to get prequalified for a mortgage. This involves providing basic information about your income, debts, and assets to a lender, who will then estimate the loan amount you may qualify for. Prequalification gives you an idea of how much you can borrow and helps you set a budget for your home search.

2. Mortgage Application: Once you find a property you want to purchase, you will need to submit a formal mortgage application to the lender. You will be required to provide detailed information about your financial history, employment, assets, and debts. The

lender will use this information to assess your creditworthiness and determine if you qualify for the loan.

3. Documentation and Verification: The lender will request documentation to support the information provided in your application, such as pay stubs, bank statements, tax returns, and employment verification. They will also run a credit check to assess your credit history and score.

4. Mortgage Underwriting: After reviewing your application and supporting documents, the lender will initiate the underwriting process. This involves evaluating your financial situation, the property's value, and the loan-to-value ratio. The underwriter will assess your creditworthiness, income stability, and ability to repay the loan. They may request additional documents or clarification during this stage.

5. Loan Approval and Offer: If your application meets the lender's criteria, they will issue a loan approval letter, stating the terms and conditions of the mortgage offer. This includes the loan amount, interest rate, repayment term, and any other applicable fees or conditions. You will have the opportunity to review and accept the offer.

6. Property Appraisal: The lender will arrange for a professional appraisal of the property to determine its market value. This is to ensure that the property is worth the amount being financed and serves as collateral for the loan.

7. Closing and Funding: Once all the necessary approvals and documentation are in place, a closing date will be scheduled. At the closing, you will sign the final loan documents, including the mortgage agreement and other legal disclosures. You will also pay any closing costs and fees. After the closing, the lender will fund the loan, and you will officially become the homeowner.

8. Repayment: Once the mortgage is funded, you will begin making monthly mortgage payments as outlined in the loan agreement. This

includes principal and interest payments, as well as any escrow payments for property taxes and insurance.

It's important to note that the mortgage process can vary slightly depending on the lender, type of mortgage, and local regulations. Working with a knowledgeable mortgage professional can help guide you through the process and ensure a smooth experience.

**Types of mortgages and their pros and cons**

There are several types of mortgages available, each with its own set of pros and cons. Here are some common types of mortgages:

1. Conventional Mortgage:
   - Pros: Conventional mortgages typically offer competitive interest rates and flexible terms. They are not backed by the government, so they may have fewer restrictions.
   - Cons: Conventional mortgages often require a higher credit score and a larger down payment compared to other types of mortgages.

2. FHA (Federal Housing Administration) Mortgage:
   - Pros: FHA mortgages are insured by the government, allowing borrowers with lower credit scores and smaller down payments to qualify. They often have more flexible lending criteria.
   - Cons: FHA mortgages require mortgage insurance premiums (MIP), which can increase the overall cost of the loan. Borrowers may also face certain property restrictions.

3. VA (Veterans Affairs) Mortgage:
   - Pros: VA mortgages are available to eligible veterans, active-duty service members, and surviving spouses. They offer competitive interest rates, no down payment requirement, and no mortgage insurance.
   - Cons: VA mortgages are only available to those who meet specific eligibility criteria. Borrowers may need to pay a funding fee, and certain property restrictions may apply.

4. USDA (United States Department of Agriculture) Mortgage:

- Pros: USDA mortgages are designed to assist low- to moderate-income borrowers in rural areas. They offer low-interest rates, no down payment requirement, and flexible credit requirements.
- Cons: USDA mortgages are only available for properties located in eligible rural areas. Borrowers may need to pay mortgage insurance premiums (PMI).

5. Adjustable Rate Mortgage (ARM):
- Pros: ARMs typically offer a lower initial interest rate compared to fixed-rate mortgages. They can be beneficial if you plan to move or refinance before the rate adjusts.
- Cons: ARMs have an adjustable interest rate that can increase over time. This can lead to higher monthly payments and potentially more overall interest paid.

6. Fixed-Rate Mortgage:
- Pros: Fixed-rate mortgages offer stability and predictability as the interest rate remains constant throughout the loan term. Monthly payments remain the same, making budgeting easier.
- Cons: Fixed-rate mortgages may have slightly higher interest rates compared to adjustable-rate mortgages. Refinancing may be required to take advantage of lower rates in the future.

It's important to consider your financial situation, long-term plans, and personal preferences when choosing a mortgage type. Consulting with a mortgage professional can help you understand the specific pros and cons of each option and determine which one aligns best with your needs.

**Key terms and concepts related to mortgages**

Here are some key terms and concepts related to mortgages:

1. Mortgage: A loan provided by a lender, typically a bank or financial institution, to finance the purchase of a property. The property serves as collateral for the loan.

2. Interest Rate: The percentage of the loan amount that the borrower pays to the lender as additional cost for borrowing the money. It

determines the cost of borrowing and affects the monthly mortgage payment.

3. Down Payment: The initial payment made by the borrower towards the purchase price of the property. It is usually expressed as a percentage of the total purchase price. A higher down payment can result in better loan terms.

4. Loan Term: The length of time over which the mortgage loan is repaid. Common loan terms are 15, 20, or 30 years. A longer loan term generally results in lower monthly payments but higher overall interest paid.

5. Amortization: The process of gradually paying off the mortgage loan through regular monthly payments. Each payment includes both principal (the loan amount) and interest.

6. Principal: The original loan amount borrowed from the lender. As the borrower makes mortgage payments, the principal gradually decreases.

7. Closing Costs: The fees and expenses associated with the purchase of a property and the mortgage loan. These may include appraisal fees, title insurance, attorney fees, and loan origination fees.

8. Private Mortgage Insurance (PMI): Insurance required by lenders when the down payment is less than 20% of the property's purchase price. It protects the lender in case the borrower defaults on the loan.

9. Escrow: An account held by the lender to collect and disburse funds for property taxes, homeowners insurance, and mortgage insurance. The borrower pays a portion of these expenses with each monthly mortgage payment.

10. Pre-approval: The process of getting a preliminary commitment from a lender for a mortgage loan. It involves submitting financial documents and credit information to determine the loan amount for which the borrower qualifies.

Understanding these key terms and concepts can help you navigate the mortgage process and make informed decisions when purchasing a property. It's always advisable to consult with a mortgage professional who can provide personalized guidance based on your specific financial situation and goals.

## 3.    Assessing Your Financial Situation

### Evaluating your current financial position

When evaluating your current financial position for the purpose of getting a mortgage, there are some specific factors to consider. Here are key areas to focus on:

1. Credit Score: Lenders consider your credit score as an indicator of your creditworthiness. A higher credit score usually leads to better mortgage terms and interest rates. Check your credit score and take steps to improve it if necessary, such as paying bills on time, reducing debt, and correcting any errors on your credit report.

2. Income and Employment Stability: Lenders want to ensure that you have a stable income to make mortgage payments. Evaluate your income sources and determine if they are consistent and reliable. Additionally, lenders typically prefer borrowers who have been employed for a certain period, so consider your employment history as well.

3. Debt-to-Income Ratio: Calculate your debt-to-income ratio by dividing your monthly debt payments by your gross monthly income. Lenders generally prefer a lower ratio, as it indicates that you have enough income to cover your debt obligations and mortgage payments.

4. Down Payment: Determine how much you can afford to put towards a down payment. A larger down payment can help you secure a better interest rate and reduce the amount you need to borrow. Saving for a down payment demonstrates financial discipline and stability to lenders.

5. Savings and Reserves: Lenders may also consider your savings and reserves when evaluating your financial position. Having savings not only shows your ability to handle unexpected expenses but also provides a safety net in case of financial difficulties.

6. Debt and Financial Obligations: Consider your existing debt, such as student loans, credit card balances, and car loans. Lenders will factor in your debt load when assessing your ability to manage mortgage payments.

7. Affordability: Evaluate your monthly budget to determine how much you can comfortably afford for mortgage payments. Consider other housing-related expenses, such as property taxes, insurance, and maintenance costs.

8. Documentation: Gather the necessary documents, such as pay stubs, tax returns, bank statements, and proof of assets, to demonstrate your financial stability and ability to afford a mortgage.

9. Pre-Approval: Consider getting pre-approved for a mortgage. This will provide you with an estimate of the loan amount you can qualify for, helping you set realistic expectations and narrow down your home search.

It is also advisable to consult with a mortgage professional who can provide personalized guidance based on your specific financial situation and goals. They can help evaluate your financial position, assess your borrowing capacity, and guide you through the mortgage application process.

**Determining your budget and affordability**

Determining your budget and affordability for a mortgage is an important step in the homebuying process. Here are some key factors to consider:

1. Income: Start by evaluating your monthly income. Calculate your total income from all sources, including salaries, bonuses, commissions, and any other regular income. This will give you a

baseline for how much you can allocate towards your mortgage payment.

2. Expenses: Take a close look at your monthly expenses. Consider your fixed expenses like utilities, insurance, transportation costs, and any other regular payments. Also, consider your variable expenses like groceries, entertainment, and discretionary spending. Subtract your total expenses from your monthly income to determine how much you have available for your mortgage payment.

3. Down Payment: Determine how much you can afford to put towards a down payment. The larger the down payment, the lower your monthly mortgage payment will be. Aim for a down payment of at least 20% to avoid private mortgage insurance (PMI) and potentially secure better loan terms.

4. Mortgage Payments: Use a mortgage calculator to estimate your monthly mortgage payments. Consider factors such as the loan amount, interest rate, and loan term. Keep in mind that your mortgage payment will include not only the principal and interest but also property taxes, homeowner's insurance, and possibly mortgage insurance.

5. Debt-to-Income Ratio: Calculate your debt-to-income (DTI) ratio by dividing your total monthly debt payments (including your estimated mortgage payment) by your gross monthly income. Lenders typically prefer a DTI ratio of 43% or lower. A lower DTI ratio indicates that you have more disposable income available to cover your mortgage payment.

6. Consider Other Expenses: Remember to factor in additional homeownership expenses such as property taxes, homeowner's association (HOA) fees, maintenance costs, and any potential renovations or repairs. These expenses can significantly impact your overall budget.

7. Future Financial Goals: Consider your long-term financial goals when determining your affordability. Think about other financial priorities such as saving for retirement, education, or emergencies.

It's important to strike a balance between your mortgage payments and your other financial goals.

8. Pre-Approval: Consider getting pre-approved for a mortgage. This will give you a better understanding of the loan amount you qualify for and the interest rate you can secure. It will also help you set a realistic budget and narrow down your home search.

Remember that it's crucial to be realistic and conservative when determining your budget and affordability. It's better to have some breathing room in your budget rather than stretching yourself too thin. Consulting with a mortgage professional can provide valuable insights and guidance specific to your financial situation and goals.

### Calculating your debt-to-income ratio

Calculating your debt-to-income (DTI) ratio is an important step in determining your eligibility for a mortgage. Here's how you can calculate it:

1. Determine your monthly gross income: Add up all of your gross monthly income, including salaries, wages, bonuses, commissions, and any other regular income sources.

2. Calculate your total monthly debt payments: Add up all of your monthly debt payments, including student loans, car loans, credit card payments, personal loans, and any other outstanding debts.

3. Divide your total monthly debt payments by your monthly gross income: Divide your total monthly debt payments by your monthly gross income. Multiply the result by 100 to convert it to a percentage.

DTI Ratio = (Total Monthly Debt Payments / Monthly Gross Income) x 100

For example, if your total monthly debt payments amount to $1,500 and your monthly gross income is $5,000, your DTI ratio would be:

DTI Ratio = ($1,500 / $5,000) x 100 = 30%

Lenders typically prefer a DTI ratio of 43% or lower. A lower DTI ratio indicates that you have more disposable income available to cover your mortgage payment.

It's important to note that different lenders may have different guidelines and requirements regarding DTI ratios. Some lenders may be more flexible depending on other factors such as credit score and down payment amount. It's always best to consult with a mortgage professional who can provide personalized advice based on your specific financial situation and goals.

## 4.     Building a Strong Credit Profile

### Importance of a good credit score for mortgage approval

Having a good credit score is crucial when it comes to mortgage approval. Here are some reasons why a good credit score is important:

1. Loan eligibility: A good credit score increases your chances of being approved for a mortgage loan. Lenders use your credit score to assess your creditworthiness and determine the level of risk in lending to you. A higher credit score indicates that you have a history of responsibly managing your debts, making you a more attractive borrower.

2. Interest rates: A good credit score can help you secure a lower interest rate on your mortgage loan. Lenders offer better interest rates to borrowers with higher credit scores because they consider them to be less risky. Even a small difference in interest rates can significantly impact the overall cost of your mortgage over time, potentially saving you thousands of dollars.

3. Loan terms: A good credit score can also influence the terms of your mortgage loan. Lenders may be more willing to offer favorable terms, such as a higher loan amount or a longer repayment period, to borrowers with good credit. This can give you more flexibility and affordability in managing your mortgage payments.

4. Mortgage insurance: If you have a lower credit score, you may be required to pay for private mortgage insurance (PMI) in addition to your mortgage payments. PMI is typically required for borrowers with a down payment of less than 20% of the home's purchase price. Having a good credit score may help you avoid the additional cost of PMI.

5. Future borrowing opportunities: A good credit score not only helps with mortgage approval but also opens doors for other borrowing opportunities in the future. Whether it's getting a car loan, applying for a credit card, or securing a personal loan, a strong credit score demonstrates your creditworthiness and can lead to more favorable terms and conditions.

It's important to regularly monitor your credit score and take steps to maintain or improve it. This includes paying bills on time, keeping credit card balances low, and avoiding new debt unless necessary. By maintaining a good credit score, you can increase your chances of mortgage approval and enjoy the benefits of more favorable loan terms.

**Tips for improving and maintaining a high credit score**

Improving and maintaining a high credit score takes time and discipline. Here are some tips to help you improve and maintain a good credit score:

1. Pay your bills on time: Payment history is one of the most important factors in calculating your credit score. Make sure to pay all your bills, including credit card bills, loans, and utilities, on time. Late payments can have a negative impact on your credit score.

2. Keep your credit card balances low: Aim to keep your credit card balances below 30% of your credit limit. High credit card utilization can negatively affect your credit score. Paying off your balances in full each month is ideal, but if that's not possible, try to make more than the minimum payment.

3. Don't apply for too much new credit at once: When you apply for new credit, it can result in a hard inquiry on your credit report, which

can temporarily lower your credit score. Avoid opening multiple new accounts within a short period of time. Instead, focus on using and managing your existing credit responsibly.

4. Maintain a mix of credit types: Having a diverse mix of credit types, such as credit cards, loans, and a mortgage, can positively impact your credit score. However, only take on new credit if you actually need it and can manage it responsibly.

5. Regularly review your credit report: Obtain a free copy of your credit report from each of the major credit bureaus (Equifax, Experian, and TransUnion) once a year and review it for any errors or discrepancies. If you find any inaccuracies, report them and have them corrected promptly.

6. Avoid closing old credit accounts: Length of credit history is an important factor in determining your credit score. If you have old credit accounts with no negative history, it's generally beneficial to keep them open. Closing old accounts can shorten your credit history and potentially lower your score.

7. Be cautious with credit applications: Before applying for credit, do your research and compare offers. Applying for too much credit within a short period can raise concerns for lenders and negatively impact your credit score.

8. Use credit responsibly: Use credit as a tool to build a positive credit history. Make regular payments, avoid maxing out credit cards, and only borrow what you can afford to repay.

Remember, improving and maintaining a good credit score is a gradual process. It requires responsible financial habits and consistent effort over time. By following these tips, you can work towards a better credit score and enjoy the benefits that come with it.

**Strategies for managing debt and paying off outstanding loans**

Managing debt and paying off outstanding loans can be challenging, but with a well-planned strategy, it is achievable. Here are some strategies to help you effectively manage your debt and pay off your outstanding loans:

1. Create a budget: Start by creating a comprehensive budget that includes all of your income and expenses. This will help you understand your financial situation and identify areas where you can cut back on expenses to free up money for debt repayment.

2. Prioritize your debts: Make a list of all your debts, including outstanding loans and credit card balances. Prioritize them based on factors such as interest rates and outstanding balances. Consider paying off high-interest debts first to minimize the amount of interest you pay over time.

3. Snowball or avalanche method: There are two popular methods for paying off debts: the snowball method and the avalanche method. With the snowball method, you start by paying off the smallest debt first while making minimum payments on other debts. Once the smallest debt is paid off, you move on to the next smallest debt. This method provides psychological motivation as you see debts being eliminated. The avalanche method, on the other hand, focuses on paying off debts with the highest interest rates first. This method can save you more money on interest in the long run.

4. Negotiate lower interest rates: Contact your creditors and lenders to negotiate lower interest rates on your loans. Lower interest rates can help you save money and pay off your debts faster. Explain your financial situation and provide reasons why they should consider lowering the interest rates.

5. Explore debt consolidation: If you have multiple debts with high-interest rates, consider consolidating them into a single loan with a lower interest rate. Debt consolidation can simplify your repayments and potentially save you money on interest. However, it's important to carefully evaluate the terms and fees associated with the consolidation loan.

6. Increase your income: Look for ways to increase your income, such as taking on a part-time job, freelancing, or selling unwanted

items. The extra income can be used to accelerate your debt repayment.

7. Cut back on expenses: Review your budget and identify areas where you can cut back on expenses. Consider reducing discretionary spending, finding cheaper alternatives for necessities, and eliminating unnecessary subscriptions or memberships. Redirect the money saved towards your debt repayment.

8. Seek professional advice if needed: If you're struggling to manage your debt on your own, consider seeking professional advice from a credit counselor or a financial advisor. They can provide personalized guidance and help you develop a debt management plan.

Remember, managing debt and paying off loans takes time and perseverance. Be consistent with your debt repayment strategy, stay focused on your goals, and celebrate small victories along the way. With determination and discipline, you can successfully manage your debt and become debt-free.

## 5.    Researching and Comparing Mortgage Options

### Researching different lenders and mortgage products

Researching different lenders and mortgage products is an essential step in finding the right mortgage for your needs. Here are some strategies to help you in your research process:

1. Determine your needs: Start by determining your specific needs and financial goals. Consider factors such as the type of property you want to purchase, your budget, desired loan term, and your credit score. Understanding your needs will help you narrow down your options and focus your research.

2. Explore different types of lenders: There are various types of lenders you can consider, including traditional banks, credit unions, mortgage brokers, and online lenders. Each type of lender has its own advantages and disadvantages, so it's important to research and understand their offerings and reputation.

3. Compare interest rates: Interest rates play a significant role in the cost of your mortgage. Research and compare the interest rates offered by different lenders. Keep in mind that interest rates can vary based on factors such as your credit score, loan term, and the type of mortgage product you choose.

4. Consider mortgage products: Familiarize yourself with the different mortgage products available in the market. Common options include fixed-rate mortgages, adjustable-rate mortgages (ARMs), government-insured loans (such as FHA or VA loans), and jumbo loans. Each product has its own features, advantages, and eligibility criteria. Evaluate which mortgage product aligns with your financial goals and preferences.

5. Review fees and closing costs: In addition to interest rates, it's important to consider the fees and closing costs associated with each lender and mortgage product. These can include origination fees, appraisal fees, title insurance, and more. Compare the fees and closing costs of different lenders to ensure you have a clear understanding of the overall costs.

6. Read customer reviews and ratings: Research customer reviews and ratings for the lenders you are considering. This can provide insights into their customer service, responsiveness, and overall customer satisfaction. Websites such as Better Business Bureau, Consumer Financial Protection Bureau, and online review platforms can be helpful resources.

7. Seek recommendations and advice: Reach out to friends, family, or colleagues who have recently gone through the mortgage process. They may be able to provide recommendations or share their experiences with particular lenders or mortgage products. Additionally, consider consulting with a mortgage broker or

financial advisor who can provide expert advice based on your specific situation.

8. Pre-approval process: Once you have identified potential lenders, consider going through the pre-approval process. This involves submitting your financial information and documentation to the lender for review. Pre-approval can give you a clearer understanding of the loan amount you qualify for and can help you negotiate with sellers.

Remember to take your time during the research process and ask questions to ensure you fully understand the terms and conditions of each lender and mortgage product. By conducting thorough research and comparing your options, you'll be better equipped to make an informed decision and find the right lender and mortgage product for your needs.

**Understanding interest rates, fees, and loan terms**

Understanding interest rates, fees, and loan terms is crucial when researching and comparing mortgage products. Here's a breakdown of each concept:

1. Interest Rates: Interest rates determine the cost of borrowing money for your mortgage. They are expressed as a percentage and can be either fixed or adjustable.

   - Fixed-rate mortgage: With a fixed-rate mortgage, the interest rate remains the same throughout the loan term. This provides stability and predictable monthly payments.

   - Adjustable-rate mortgage (ARM): An ARM has an interest rate that can fluctuate over time. Typically, the initial rate is lower than that of a fixed-rate mortgage, but it can increase or decrease based on market conditions. ARMs usually have a fixed rate for an initial period (e.g., 5, 7, or 10 years) before adjusting.

   It's important to compare interest rates from different lenders to find the most favorable terms for your situation. Keep in mind that rates can vary based on factors like credit score, loan amount, and loan term.

2. Fees: Mortgage fees are charges associated with the loan process. They can include:

- Origination fees: These are fees charged by the lender for processing and underwriting the loan.

- Appraisal fees: Lenders require an appraisal to determine the value of the property, and this fee covers the cost of the appraisal.

- Title insurance: This protects the lender and buyer from any potential issues with the property's title, such as liens or ownership disputes.

- Closing costs: These include various fees related to the closing of the loan, such as attorney fees, recording fees, and prepaid property taxes or insurance.

Be sure to review the Loan Estimate and Closing Disclosure provided by the lender, which outline all the fees associated with the loan. Comparing these fees across different lenders will help you understand the overall cost of the mortgage.

3. Loan Terms: Loan terms refer to the duration of the mortgage and the repayment schedule. Common loan terms are 15, 20, or 30 years, although other options may be available.

- Shorter loan terms: Shorter loan terms (e.g., 15 years) typically have lower interest rates but higher monthly payments. They result in less interest paid over the life of the loan and faster equity buildup.

- Longer loan terms: Longer loan terms (e.g., 30 years) generally have higher interest rates but lower monthly payments. They spread the cost of the loan over a longer period, resulting in more interest paid overall.

It's important to consider your financial goals and budget when selecting a loan term. Evaluate the impact of different loan terms on your monthly payments and the total interest paid over time.

By understanding interest rates, fees, and loan terms, you can make an informed decision when comparing mortgage products. Take the time to carefully review and compare these factors from different lenders to find the mortgage that best fits your financial situation and goals.

**Using online tools and resources to compare mortgage offers**

Using online tools and resources can be a convenient and efficient way to compare mortgage offers. Here are some steps to help you navigate through the process:

1. Research reputable websites: Start by identifying reputable websites that provide mortgage comparison tools. Look for websites that offer comprehensive information, user-friendly interfaces, and access to multiple lenders.

2. Gather necessary information: Before using an online tool, gather relevant information about your financial situation and the specific loan you're looking for. This may include your credit score, income, desired loan amount, and loan term. Having this information readily available will make the comparison process smoother.

3. Utilize mortgage calculators: Many websites offer mortgage calculators that allow you to input your information and receive estimates of monthly payments, interest rates, and total costs for different loan options. These calculators can help you get a sense of how different factors impact the overall cost of the loan.

4. Compare interest rates: Use the online tools to compare interest rates from different lenders. Look for the Annual Percentage Rate (APR), which includes both the interest rate and any additional fees. Remember to compare rates for the same loan type, term, and loan amount to get an accurate comparison.

5. Consider additional fees and costs: Look beyond the interest rate and consider the additional fees and costs associated with each mortgage offer. This includes origination fees, closing costs, and any other fees disclosed by the lender. Some online tools provide a breakdown of these costs, allowing you to compare them side by side.

6. Read reviews and customer experiences: Take the time to read reviews and customer experiences with the lenders you are considering. This will give you insights into their reputation, customer service, and overall satisfaction levels.

7. Get personalized quotes: Once you've narrowed down your options using online tools, reach out to the lenders directly to get personalized quotes. This will ensure that the information you receive is tailored to your specific situation and can help you make a final decision.

Remember to approach online tools as a starting point for your research. It's always a good idea to consult with a mortgage professional or financial advisor who can provide personalized advice and guidance based on your unique circumstances.

## 6.      Negotiating with Lenders

### Strategies for negotiating lower interest rates and fees

Negotiating lower interest rates and fees on your mortgage can save you a significant amount of money over the life of the loan. Here are some strategies to help you in the negotiation process:

1. Research and compare rates: Before negotiating, do your research and compare interest rates and fees from different lenders. This will give you leverage when negotiating with your preferred lender, as you can reference competitive offers.

2. Improve your credit score: A higher credit score can give you more negotiating power. Take steps to improve your credit score by paying bills on time, reducing your overall debt, and correcting any

errors on your credit report. A better credit score may help you qualify for lower interest rates.

3. Gather documentation of your financial stability: Lenders want to see that you are a low-risk borrower. Gather documentation of your stable income, employment history, and financial assets. This can help you negotiate for better terms.

4. Highlight your loyalty: If you have been a long-term customer with the lender or have multiple accounts with them, mention this during negotiations. Lenders may be more willing to offer you lower rates and fees to retain your business.

5. Negotiate based on market conditions: Keep an eye on the current market conditions and interest rate trends. If the market is favorable for borrowers, use this as leverage to negotiate for lower rates and fees.

6. Consider paying points: Points are upfront fees paid to the lender in exchange for a lower interest rate. Depending on your financial situation and how long you plan to stay in the home, paying points may be a viable option to negotiate a lower interest rate.

7. Ask for lender credits: In addition to negotiating interest rates, you can also negotiate for lender credits. These credits can be used to offset closing costs and other fees associated with the mortgage.

8. Seek multiple quotes: Don't be afraid to shop around and get multiple quotes from different lenders. This will give you more options to compare and negotiate for the best terms.

9. Work with a mortgage broker: Consider working with a mortgage broker who has access to multiple lenders. They can help you negotiate on your behalf and find the best rates and fees for your specific situation.

Remember, negotiation is a two-way process. Be prepared to make compromises and find a middle ground that benefits both you and the lender. It's always a good idea to consult with a mortgage professional or financial advisor who can provide personalized advice and guidance during the negotiation process.

## Tips for leveraging your financial strengths during negotiations

When negotiating, leveraging your financial strengths can give you an advantage and help you achieve more favorable terms. Here are some tips for leveraging your financial strengths during negotiations:

1. Highlight your positive cash flow: If you have a consistent and positive cash flow, emphasize this during negotiations. It shows that you have the financial stability to meet your obligations and are less likely to default.

2. Showcase your savings: Having a significant amount of savings can demonstrate your financial responsibility and ability to handle unexpected expenses. Highlight your savings during negotiations to show that you have a cushion in case of emergencies.

3. Demonstrate a strong credit history: A good credit history indicates your reliability in repaying debts. Provide evidence of your on-time payments, low credit utilization, and a diverse credit mix. This can give you leverage when negotiating for lower interest rates or fees.

4. Emphasize your low debt-to-income ratio: A low debt-to-income ratio shows that you have a manageable level of debt compared to your income. This indicates that you are financially responsible and have the capacity to take on additional debt without strain.

5. Show your investment portfolio: If you have a well-diversified investment portfolio, mention it during negotiations. It demonstrates your financial knowledge and success in managing your investments, which can enhance your credibility and negotiating position.

6. Offer a larger down payment: A larger down payment reduces the lender's risk and may make them more willing to negotiate better terms. If possible, offer a larger down payment to showcase your financial strength and commitment to the transaction.

7. Leverage your existing relationships: If you have a long-standing relationship with the lender or financial institution, mention it during negotiations. Existing relationships can give you an edge and make the lender more willing to offer you favorable terms to maintain your business.

8. Use pre-approval as leverage: If you have been pre-approved for a loan, it gives you credibility and shows that you are a serious buyer. Use your pre-approval status as leverage during negotiations to demonstrate your financial readiness.

9. Be prepared to walk away: If you have strong financial strengths and options, be prepared to walk away if the terms offered are not satisfactory. This shows that you are not desperate and have other alternatives.

Remember, while leveraging your financial strengths can be advantageous, it's important to approach negotiations with respect, professionalism, and a willingness to find a mutually beneficial solution.

**Understanding lender incentives and promotions**

Understanding lender incentives and promotions can help you make informed decisions when seeking financial products or negotiating with lenders. Here are some key points to consider:

1. Competitive advantage: Lenders often offer incentives and promotions to gain a competitive edge in the market. They use these strategies to attract new customers, retain existing ones, and increase their loan or credit portfolio.

2. Lower interest rates: One common incentive is offering lower interest rates. Lenders may temporarily reduce their rates to entice borrowers and make their products more appealing. It's important to carefully review the terms and conditions, as these promotional rates may be subject to change after a specific period.

3. Fee waivers: Lenders may waive certain fees as part of their promotions. These could include application fees, origination fees,

or annual fees. By eliminating or reducing these charges, lenders aim to reduce the upfront costs for borrowers and make their products more attractive.

4. Cashback offers: Some lenders offer cashback incentives, where they provide a certain percentage of the loan amount as cashback to borrowers. This can be a valuable benefit, especially for larger loans, as it provides immediate funds that can be used for various purposes.

5. Rewards programs: Lenders may have rewards programs that offer points, discounts, or other benefits to borrowers. These programs are designed to encourage customer loyalty and provide additional value beyond the loan or credit product.

6. Flexible repayment options: Incentives can also come in the form of flexible repayment options. Lenders may offer deferred payment periods, interest-only periods, or the ability to customize repayment schedules based on the borrower's needs. These options can provide financial flexibility and make the loan more manageable.

7. Bundled services: Some lenders may offer bundled services or products as incentives. For example, a mortgage lender might offer a discounted rate on home insurance or provide access to financial planning services. These additional offerings can enhance the overall value proposition for borrowers.

8. Limited-time promotions: Many lender incentives and promotions have a limited duration. They may be available for a specific period or to a limited number of borrowers. It's important to stay updated on current promotions and take advantage of them while they are available.

9. Eligibility criteria: Lender incentives and promotions often have specific eligibility criteria. These can include factors such as credit score, income level, loan amount, or relationship status with the lender. Make sure to understand the requirements and determine if you meet them before pursuing the offer.

10. Read the fine print: Before accepting any lender incentive or promotion, carefully read the terms and conditions. Pay attention to

any potential limitations, expiration dates, or hidden fees. Understanding the details will help you make an informed decision and avoid any surprises down the line.

Remember, lender incentives and promotions are marketing strategies designed to attract customers. While they can provide benefits, it's crucial to evaluate the overall loan or credit product and consider factors beyond the incentive itself, such as interest rates, fees, and repayment terms.

## 7.    Saving for a Down Payment

**Importance of a down payment and its impact on mortgage terms**

The down payment is an important aspect of obtaining a mortgage and has a significant impact on the terms and overall cost of the loan. Here are some key points to understand:

1. Definition: A down payment is the initial payment made by the borrower when purchasing a property. It is typically a percentage of the total purchase price and is paid upfront at the time of closing.

2. Loan-to-Value (LTV) ratio: The down payment affects the Loan-to-Value ratio, which is the percentage of the property's value that the lender is financing. For example, if the down payment is 20% of the purchase price, the LTV ratio would be 80%. Lenders often have maximum LTV requirements, and a higher down payment can help borrowers meet these criteria.

3. Impact on interest rate: A larger down payment can potentially result in a lower interest rate. Lenders consider the down payment as an indicator of the borrower's financial stability and commitment to the property. With a lower risk perception, lenders may offer more favorable interest rates, which can save the borrower money over the life of the loan.

4. Private Mortgage Insurance (PMI): If the down payment is less than 20% of the purchase price, lenders often require borrowers to

pay for Private Mortgage Insurance (PMI). PMI protects the lender in case of default and adds an additional cost to the monthly mortgage payment. Avoiding PMI by making a larger down payment can help reduce the overall cost of the loan.

5. Loan amount and monthly payments: The down payment directly affects the loan amount. A larger down payment reduces the loan amount, which in turn lowers the monthly mortgage payments. This can provide more financial flexibility and reduce the burden of monthly expenses.

6. Equity and home equity loans: The down payment establishes the initial equity in the property. Equity is the difference between the market value of the property and the outstanding loan balance. A larger down payment means more equity from the start, which can be beneficial if the borrower intends to access home equity in the future through a home equity loan or line of credit.

7. Impact on affordability: The down payment affects the affordability of a home purchase. A larger down payment means a smaller loan amount, which can make it easier to qualify for a mortgage and afford the monthly payments. It also reduces the risk of being house-poor, where a significant portion of income goes towards housing costs.

8. Long-term savings: Making a larger down payment can lead to long-term savings. By reducing the loan amount and potentially securing a lower interest rate, borrowers can save on interest payments over the life of the loan. This can translate into thousands of dollars in savings.

9. Personal financial goals: The down payment amount should align with your personal financial goals and circumstances. While a 20% down payment is often recommended to avoid PMI, there are loan programs available for borrowers with lower down payments. It's essential to consider your financial situation, future plans, and the trade-offs between a larger down payment and other financial priorities.

In conclusion, the down payment plays a crucial role in mortgage terms and affordability. A larger down payment can lead to better loan terms, lower interest rates, reduced monthly payments, and long-term savings. It also provides more equity and improves the borrower's financial position. It's important to carefully consider your financial situation and goals when determining the appropriate down payment amount for your mortgage.

**Strategies for saving money for a down payment**

Saving money for a down payment requires discipline and a solid financial plan. Here are some strategies to help you save effectively:

1. Set a savings goal: Determine the amount you need to save for your desired down payment. Research the housing market to understand the price range of properties you are interested in, and calculate the down payment based on the percentage required by lenders (typically 20% is recommended to avoid PMI). Having a specific savings goal will help you stay focused and motivated.

2. Create a budget: Evaluate your monthly income and expenses to determine how much you can save each month. Create a detailed budget that includes all your expenses, such as rent, utilities, groceries, transportation, and entertainment. Identify areas where you can cut back on expenses and allocate more towards your down payment savings.

3. Automate savings: Set up an automatic transfer from your checking account to a designated savings account specifically for your down payment. By automating the process, you ensure that a portion of your income is consistently saved without the temptation to spend it.

4. Reduce unnecessary expenses: Take a close look at your spending habits and identify areas where you can cut back. Consider reducing discretionary expenses like dining out, entertainment, shopping, and subscriptions. Channel those savings directly into your down payment fund.

5. Increase your income: Explore opportunities to increase your income. This could involve taking on a side job, freelancing, or starting a small business. Use the additional income solely for your down payment savings.

6. Save windfalls and bonuses: Whenever you receive unexpected income, such as tax refunds, work bonuses, or monetary gifts, resist the urge to spend it and instead, deposit it directly into your down payment savings.

7. Cut housing costs: Consider downsizing your living arrangements or finding a more affordable rental option. By reducing your monthly housing costs, you can save more towards your down payment.

8. Save windfalls and bonuses: Whenever you receive unexpected income, such as tax refunds, work bonuses, or monetary gifts, resist the urge to spend it and instead, deposit it directly into your down payment savings.

9. Explore down payment assistance programs: Research if there are any government or local programs that offer down payment assistance for first-time homebuyers. These programs can provide grants or low-interest loans to help bridge the gap between your savings and the required down payment amount.

10. Stay motivated and track progress: Keep your goal in mind and stay motivated throughout the saving process. Regularly track your progress by reviewing your savings account balance and updating your budget. Celebrate milestones along the way to keep yourself motivated and focused on the end goal.

Remember, saving for a down payment takes time and commitment. By implementing these strategies and staying consistent, you can steadily build your down payment fund and work towards achieving your homeownership goals.

**Exploring alternative down payment options and assistance programs**

If saving up for a down payment seems challenging, there are alternative options and assistance programs that can help you achieve your goal of homeownership. Here are some options to consider:

1. Low down payment mortgage programs: Some lenders offer mortgage programs that require a lower down payment than the traditional 20%. For example, you may find lenders who offer loans with down payments as low as 3% or 5%. However, keep in mind that lower down payments often come with additional costs, such as private mortgage insurance (PMI) or a higher interest rate.

2. FHA loans: The Federal Housing Administration (FHA) provides loans with a down payment requirement as low as 3.5%. These loans are backed by the government and are available to borrowers with lower credit scores. However, FHA loans also require mortgage insurance premiums (MIP) throughout the life of the loan.

3. VA loans: If you are a current or former member of the military, you may qualify for a VA loan. These loans are backed by the Department of Veterans Affairs and often require no down payment. VA loans also typically have lower interest rates and do not require mortgage insurance.

4. USDA loans: The United States Department of Agriculture (USDA) offers loans for rural and suburban homebuyers. These loans require no down payment and have favorable interest rates. However, USDA loans have specific eligibility requirements based on income and the location of the property.

5. Down payment assistance programs: Many state and local governments, as well as non-profit organizations, offer down payment assistance programs to help first-time homebuyers. These programs provide grants, loans, or forgivable loans that can be used towards the down payment or closing costs. Research the programs available in your area to see if you qualify.

6. Employer assistance programs: Some employers offer down payment assistance as part of their employee benefits package. These

programs may provide grants or loans to help employees with their down payment. Check with your human resources department to see if your employer offers any homeownership assistance programs.

7. Gift from family or friends: If you have family or friends who are willing and able to help, they can gift you the funds for your down payment. Lenders typically allow gift funds to be used as long as there is documentation to verify the source of the funds.

8. Rent-to-own programs: In a rent-to-own program, you rent a property with the option to buy it in the future. A portion of your rent payment is typically applied towards the down payment or purchase price. This option allows you to save up while living in the property and potentially lock in a purchase price before the market appreciates.

When exploring alternative down payment options and assistance programs, it's important to thoroughly research and understand the terms, conditions, and potential costs associated with each option. Consulting with a mortgage professional or housing counselor can provide valuable guidance and help you determine the best option for your specific situation.

## 8.    Managing Closing Costs

### Understanding closing costs and their breakdown

Closing costs are the fees and expenses that homebuyers incur during the process of purchasing a property. These costs are typically paid at the closing of the real estate transaction. Here is a breakdown of some common closing costs:

1. Loan-Related Costs:
   - Origination Fee: This is a fee charged by the lender for processing the loan application.
   - Discount Points: These are optional fees paid to the lender in exchange for a lower interest rate on the mortgage.
   - Appraisal Fee: This fee covers the cost of assessing the value of the property.

- Credit Report Fee: Lenders charge this fee to obtain your credit report.
- Loan Processing Fee: This fee covers the administrative costs of processing your loan.
- Underwriting Fee: This fee is charged by the lender for evaluating and approving your loan application.

2. Title-Related Costs:
- Title Search and Insurance: These fees ensure that the property's title is clear and provide protection against any ownership disputes or liens.
- Title Examination Fee: This fee is charged for reviewing public records to confirm the property's legal ownership and any encumbrances.
- Title Insurance Binder: This fee covers the temporary insurance policy until the final title insurance policy is issued.

3. Government Fees:
- Recording Fees: These fees are paid to the county or municipality for recording the deed and other legal documents related to the property.
- Transfer Taxes: Some states and localities charge taxes on property transfers.

4. Prepaid Expenses:
- Property Taxes: Depending on when the property taxes are due, you may need to prepay a portion of them at closing.
- Homeowners Insurance: Lenders often require you to prepay the first year's insurance premium at closing.
- Prepaid Interest: This covers the interest that accrues on your mortgage from the closing date to the end of the month.

5. Miscellaneous Costs:
- Home Inspection: This fee is for a professional inspection of the property to identify any potential issues.
- Survey Fee: If a survey is required, this fee covers the cost of measuring and mapping the property boundaries.
- Attorney Fees: In some states, an attorney may be involved in the closing process to review legal documents.

It's important to note that closing costs can vary depending on factors such as the property location, purchase price, loan amount, and the specific terms negotiated with the lender. It's advisable to request a Loan Estimate from your lender, which provides an estimate of the closing costs you can expect to pay. Additionally, working with a real estate agent and seeking guidance from a mortgage professional can help you navigate the closing process and understand the breakdown of costs specific to your situation.

**Tips for negotiating and minimizing closing costs**

Negotiating and minimizing closing costs can help you save money when purchasing a property. Here are some tips to consider:

1. Shop Around for Lenders: Different lenders may offer different closing costs. Obtain quotes from multiple lenders and compare their fees and rates. This will give you leverage when negotiating with lenders.

2. Request a Loan Estimate: Ask each lender for a Loan Estimate, which provides an itemized breakdown of the closing costs. Review the estimates carefully and compare them to identify any discrepancies or excessive fees.

3. Negotiate with the Seller: In some cases, sellers may be willing to contribute towards the buyer's closing costs. This can help reduce your out-of-pocket expenses. Discuss this possibility with your real estate agent and include it as part of your negotiation strategy.

4. Consider Different Loan Options: Different loan programs have varying closing costs. Explore different loan options to see if there are programs with lower fees or special incentives for first-time buyers or veterans.

5. Review and Negotiate Third-Party Fees: Some closing costs, such as appraisal fees or title insurance, may be set by third-party providers. Ask for a breakdown of these fees and see if you can negotiate or find alternative providers with more competitive rates.

6. Understand and Challenge Fees: Take the time to review each closing cost item and ask for clarification on any fees that seem unclear or excessive. If you find any errors or questionable charges, don't hesitate to question or negotiate them with the lender.

7. Consider a No-Closing-Cost Loan: Some lenders offer the option of a no-closing-cost loan, where the closing costs are rolled into the loan amount or financed in some other way. While this may increase your monthly mortgage payment, it can help minimize upfront expenses.

8. Timing Matters: Discuss the closing date with the seller and your lender. Closing towards the end of the month can help reduce prepaid interest and property tax expenses.

9. Work with an Experienced Real Estate Agent: A knowledgeable real estate agent can guide you through the negotiation process and provide insights on how to minimize closing costs. They can also help you identify potential cost-saving opportunities.

Remember, it's important to strike a balance between negotiating for lower closing costs and ensuring that you are working with reputable service providers. Be sure to read and understand all the terms and conditions associated with the closing costs before making any decisions.

**Exploring potential cost-saving options during the closing process**

When it comes to exploring potential cost-saving options during the closing process, there are several strategies you can consider. Here are a few:

1. Negotiate the Purchase Price: One of the most effective ways to save on closing costs is to negotiate a lower purchase price for the property. A lower purchase price means a lower loan amount, which can result in reduced closing costs.

2. Shop for Title Insurance: Title insurance is a crucial component of the closing process, but the cost can vary among different providers.

Shop around and compare quotes from multiple title insurance companies to find the best rate.

3. Request Fee Waivers: Some lenders or service providers may be willing to waive certain fees, especially if you have a strong credit history or are a repeat customer. It doesn't hurt to ask if any fees can be waived or reduced.

4. Utilize Seller Concessions: Depending on the negotiation, sellers may be willing to offer concessions to the buyer, such as paying for a portion of the closing costs. This can significantly reduce your out-of-pocket expenses.

5. Review Loan Documents Thoroughly: Carefully review the loan documents and closing disclosure to ensure that all fees and charges are accurate and within the agreed-upon terms. If you spot any discrepancies or unexpected charges, raise them with your lender for clarification.

6. Consider a Refinance: If you're refinancing an existing mortgage, you may be eligible for lower closing costs. Compare the costs of refinancing with different lenders to find the best deal.

7. Opt for a No-Closing-Cost Loan: As mentioned earlier, some lenders offer no-closing-cost loans, where the closing costs are rolled into the loan amount or financed in some other way. This option can help you save on upfront expenses, although it may result in a slightly higher interest rate.

8. Research Government Assistance Programs: Depending on your location and circumstances, there may be government assistance programs or grants available that can help offset some of the closing costs. Explore these options to see if you qualify.

9. Use a Homebuyer Assistance Program: Some states or municipalities offer homebuyer assistance programs that provide financial incentives or grants to help with closing costs. Research these programs and see if you're eligible to take advantage of them.

Remember, each real estate transaction is unique, and the availability of cost-saving options may vary. It's important to discuss your specific situation with your real estate agent and lender to determine the best strategies for minimizing closing costs in your particular case.

## 9.    Avoiding Costly Mistakes

### Common mistakes to avoid when applying for a home mortgage

When applying for a home mortgage, it's important to be aware of common mistakes that borrowers often make. Avoiding these mistakes can help streamline the application process and increase your chances of getting approved for a mortgage. Here are some common mistakes to avoid:

1. Not Checking Your Credit Report: Before applying for a mortgage, it's crucial to review your credit report for any errors or discrepancies. Mistakes on your credit report can lower your credit score and potentially affect your eligibility for a mortgage. Check your credit report from all three major credit bureaus (Equifax, Experian, and TransUnion) and dispute any inaccuracies you find.

2. Making Large Purchases or Applying for New Credit: Avoid making large purchases or applying for new credit before or during the mortgage application process. This includes buying a new car, furniture, or opening new credit cards. Large purchases and new credit applications can increase your debt-to-income ratio and affect your creditworthiness.

3. Not Getting Pre-Approved: Getting pre-approved for a mortgage before house hunting is essential. Pre-approval gives you a clear idea of your budget and shows sellers that you are a serious buyer. It also helps expedite the mortgage process once you find a property you want to purchase.

4. Forgetting to Compare Mortgage Rates: Shopping around for the best mortgage rate is crucial. Not comparing rates from multiple lenders can result in higher interest rates, which can significantly impact your monthly mortgage payments. Take the time to research

and compare rates from different lenders to find the most favorable terms.

5. Overlooking Hidden Costs: When budgeting for a home mortgage, it's important to consider not only the monthly mortgage payment but also the associated costs, such as property taxes, homeowners insurance, and potential homeowners association fees. Failure to account for these costs can lead to financial strain or unexpected surprises.

6. Providing Incomplete or Inaccurate Information: It's vital to provide accurate and complete information when filling out your mortgage application. Incomplete or inaccurate information can lead to delays in the approval process or even result in a denial. Double-check all the information you provide and ensure its accuracy.

7. Changing Jobs or Income: Lenders consider your employment history and income stability when evaluating your mortgage application. Changing jobs or experiencing a significant decrease in income during the application process can raise concerns for lenders. Try to maintain stable employment and income throughout the mortgage application process.

8. Not Saving Enough for the Down Payment and Closing Costs: Many mortgage programs require a down payment, and there are also closing costs to consider. Failing to save enough for these expenses can delay or hinder your ability to secure a mortgage. Start saving early and ensure you have enough funds to cover these costs.

9. Ignoring the Importance of a Good Debt-to-Income Ratio: Lenders assess your debt-to-income ratio to determine your ability to handle mortgage payments. Avoid taking on excessive debt before or during the mortgage application process. Keeping your debt-to-income ratio low can improve your chances of getting approved for a mortgage.

By avoiding these common mistakes, you can navigate the mortgage application process more effectively and increase your likelihood of securing a mortgage with favorable terms. It's always a good idea to consult with a mortgage professional who can guide you through the process and provide personalized advice based on your specific financial situation.

**Tips for navigating the mortgage application process smoothly**

Navigating the mortgage application process can be complex, but with careful planning and preparation, you can make the process smoother and increase your chances of getting approved for a mortgage. Here are some tips to help you navigate the mortgage application process smoothly:

1. Check Your Credit Score: Start by checking your credit score and reviewing your credit report. A good credit score is essential for getting approved for a mortgage. If your score is lower than desired, take steps to improve it before applying.

2. Get Pre-Approved: Getting pre-approved for a mortgage before you start house hunting can give you a clear idea of your budget and make you a more competitive buyer. It also helps streamline the application process once you find a property you want to purchase.

3. Organize Your Financial Documents: Gather all the necessary financial documents, such as tax returns, bank statements, pay stubs, and employment history. Organize them in advance to ensure a smooth application process.

4. Understand Your Budget: Determine how much you can comfortably afford to borrow and pay each month. Consider not only the mortgage payment but also other expenses like property taxes, homeowner's insurance, and maintenance costs.

5. Research Mortgage Options: Educate yourself about the different types of mortgages available and their pros and cons. This will help you choose the right mortgage product that suits your financial situation and long-term goals.

6. Shop Around for the Best Rates: Don't settle for the first mortgage offer you receive. Shop around and compare rates from multiple lenders to find the most favorable terms. Even a small difference in

interest rates can save you thousands of dollars over the life of the loan.

7. Work with a Mortgage Professional: Consider working with a mortgage professional like a loan officer or mortgage broker. They can guide you through the process, help you find suitable mortgage options, and assist with the paperwork.

8. Be Prepared for the Down Payment and Closing Costs: Save enough funds for the down payment and closing costs. Different mortgage programs have varying down payment requirements, so be aware of what is expected. Additionally, don't forget to budget for closing costs, which can include fees for appraisal, title search, and attorney services.

9. Be Responsive and Prompt: Respond to any requests or inquiries from your lender or mortgage professional promptly. Delays in providing requested documents or information can slow down the application process.

10. Avoid Major Financial Changes: During the mortgage application process, it's best to avoid making major financial changes like switching jobs, taking on new debt, or making large purchases. These changes can raise concerns for lenders and affect your eligibility.

11. Stay Informed and Ask Questions: Keep yourself informed about the progress of your mortgage application. Don't hesitate to ask questions if you have any doubts or concerns. Understanding the process will help you make informed decisions.

Remember, each mortgage application is unique, and the process may vary depending on your circumstances and the lender's requirements. By following these tips and being proactive, you can navigate the mortgage application process smoothly and increase your chances of securing a mortgage with favorable terms.

**Understanding potential risks and pitfalls**

While navigating the mortgage application process, it's important to be aware of potential risks and pitfalls that could impact your mortgage approval and overall financial well-being. Here are some key risks and pitfalls to consider:

1. High Debt-to-Income Ratio: Lenders assess your ability to repay the mortgage based on your debt-to-income ratio (DTI). If your DTI is too high, it may raise concerns about your ability to make mortgage payments. Keep your DTI within the acceptable range by managing your debts and avoiding taking on new loans or credit.

2. Inaccurate or Incomplete Documentation: Providing inaccurate or incomplete documentation can delay the mortgage approval process or even result in a denial. Double-check all the information you provide and ensure that your financial documents are accurate and up to date.

3. Not Shopping Around for the Best Mortgage Deal: Failing to shop around for the best mortgage deal can result in higher interest rates, fees, and overall costs. Take the time to compare offers from multiple lenders to find the most favorable terms that fit your financial situation.

4. Adjustable-Rate Mortgages (ARMs): While ARMs initially offer lower interest rates, they can be risky if interest rates rise in the future. Consider the potential for rate increases and assess whether you can afford the mortgage payments if rates go up.

5. Overextending Your Budget: It's crucial to have a clear understanding of your budget and not overextend yourself financially. Be realistic about what you can afford, considering not only the mortgage payment but also other expenses like property taxes, insurance, and maintenance costs.

6. Failure to Lock in an Interest Rate: If you don't lock in your interest rate, it can fluctuate until closing, potentially leading to higher monthly payments. Make sure to discuss and understand the rate lock options with your lender.

7. Property Appraisal Issues: The lender will require a property appraisal to determine its value. If the appraisal comes in lower than the purchase price, it can affect the loan amount and potentially lead to complications. Be prepared to address appraisal issues if they arise.

8. Employment Changes: Changing jobs or employment status during the mortgage application process can raise concerns for lenders. It's generally best to maintain stable employment until after you have secured the mortgage.

9. Not Budgeting for Closing Costs: Closing costs can be substantial, typically ranging from 2% to 5% of the loan amount. Failing to budget for these costs can cause financial strain. Make sure to factor in closing costs when determining your budget.

10. Ignoring the Fine Print: Carefully review all loan documents and disclosures before signing. Pay attention to the terms, conditions, fees, and any potential penalties. Seek clarification on anything you don't understand.

11. Foreclosure Risk: Failure to make mortgage payments can result in foreclosure, which can have serious long-term consequences for your credit and financial stability. Make sure you have a solid plan for meeting your mortgage obligations.

Navigating the mortgage application process with caution and understanding these potential risks and pitfalls can help you make informed decisions and increase your chances of a successful mortgage approval. Working closely with a mortgage professional can also provide valuable guidance and support throughout the process.

## 10.    Maximizing Mortgage Savings

### Strategies for reducing interest costs over the life of the mortgage

Reducing interest costs over the life of your mortgage can save you a significant amount of money. Here are some strategies to consider:

1. Make Extra Payments: Making extra payments towards your mortgage principal can help you pay off your loan faster and reduce the total interest paid. You can make additional principal payments each month or make larger lump-sum payments whenever you have extra funds available.

2. Refinance to a Lower Interest Rate: If interest rates have dropped since you initially took out your mortgage, consider refinancing to a lower interest rate. This can lower your monthly payments and reduce the total interest paid over the life of the loan. However, it's important to compare the costs associated with refinancing to ensure it makes financial sense in your situation.

3. Shorten the Loan Term: Opting for a shorter loan term, such as a 15-year mortgage instead of a 30-year mortgage, can significantly reduce the total interest paid. While the monthly payments may be higher, you'll save on interest costs in the long run.

4. Make Biweekly Payments: Instead of making one monthly payment, consider switching to biweekly payments. By doing this, you'll make 26 half-payments each year, which is equivalent to 13 full payments. This strategy can help you pay off your mortgage faster and save on interest.

5. Increase Your Monthly Payment: If you're unable to make extra payments but have some flexibility in your budget, consider increasing your monthly payment. Even a small increase can have a positive impact on reducing interest costs over time.

6. Avoid Adjustable-Rate Mortgages (ARMs): While ARMs may offer lower initial interest rates, they can increase over time, leading to higher monthly payments and potentially higher total interest costs. Opting for a fixed-rate mortgage can provide stability and predictable payments.

7. Pay Attention to Loan Terms: When selecting a mortgage, pay attention to the loan terms and conditions. Some loans may have prepayment penalties or other fees that can hinder your ability to pay

off the loan early. Choose a mortgage with favorable terms that allow for extra payments without penalties.

8. Improve Your Credit Score: A higher credit score can help you qualify for lower interest rates. Take steps to improve your credit score by paying bills on time, reducing debt, and managing your credit responsibly. Before applying for a mortgage, review your credit report and address any errors or issues.

9. Consider Mortgage Points: Mortgage points are fees paid upfront to lower the interest rate on the loan. If you have the financial means, consider paying points to reduce your interest rate and save on interest costs over time. Calculate the break-even point to determine if paying points makes financial sense for you.

10. Explore Government Programs: Research government programs that offer incentives for homeownership, such as the Federal Housing Administration (FHA) loans or VA loans for eligible veterans. These programs may offer lower interest rates or more favorable terms, reducing your overall interest costs.

Remember to consult with a mortgage professional to assess your specific financial situation and determine which strategies are most suitable for you. They can provide personalized advice and help you evaluate the potential savings and costs associated with each strategy.

## Exploring options for refinancing and loan modification

Exploring options for refinancing and loan modification can help you reduce your mortgage costs and improve your financial situation. Here are some options to consider:

1. Refinancing: Refinancing involves obtaining a new mortgage with better terms to replace your existing one. It can help you secure a lower interest rate, reduce monthly payments, or change the loan term. Here are a few types of refinancing to explore:

   a. Rate and Term Refinance: This type of refinancing aims to secure a lower interest rate or change the loan term without cashing out any equity. It can be beneficial if interest rates have dropped since you obtained your original mortgage.

b. Cash-Out Refinance: With a cash-out refinance, you borrow more than your current mortgage balance and receive the difference in cash. This can be useful if you need funds for home improvements, debt consolidation, or other financial needs. However, it's important to carefully consider the costs and potential impact on your overall financial situation.

c. Streamline Refinance: Some government-backed loan programs, such as FHA or VA loans, offer streamline refinancing options that simplify the process and require less documentation. These refinances typically have lower closing costs and may not require an appraisal.

Before pursuing refinancing, assess factors such as current interest rates, closing costs, and your financial goals. Consider working with a mortgage professional to evaluate the potential savings and determine if refinancing is the right option for you.

2. Loan Modification: Loan modification involves making changes to the terms of your existing mortgage to make it more affordable. It can be a viable option if you're facing financial hardship or struggling to make your monthly payments. Here are a few types of loan modifications to explore:

a. Interest Rate Reduction: This modification involves negotiating with your lender to lower the interest rate on your mortgage. A reduced interest rate can result in lower monthly payments and reduced overall interest costs.

b. Loan Term Extension: Extending the loan term can help lower your monthly payments by spreading them out over a longer period. However, keep in mind that this may increase the total interest paid over the life of the loan.

c. Principal Forbearance or Forgiveness: In certain circumstances, lenders may be willing to temporarily reduce or suspend a portion of your mortgage principal, or even forgive a portion of it, to help you overcome financial difficulties. This option may be available for borrowers facing severe financial hardship.

Loan modification programs and eligibility criteria vary, so it's important to reach out to your lender to discuss your specific situation. Be prepared to provide documentation of your financial hardship and demonstrate your ability to meet the modified payment terms.

3. Government Assistance Programs: Explore government assistance programs designed to help homeowners facing financial challenges. For example, the Home Affordable Refinance Program (HARP) assists homeowners with loans owned by Fannie Mae or Freddie Mac to refinance into more affordable mortgages. The Home Affordable Modification Program (HAMP) provides loan modifications for eligible borrowers.

Additionally, in response to the COVID-19 pandemic, many governments have implemented foreclosure moratoriums and introduced mortgage relief programs to support homeowners. Research and inquire about these programs to determine if you qualify for assistance.

Remember to gather all relevant financial documents and consult with a mortgage professional or housing counselor who can guide you through the refinancing or loan modification process. They can provide personalized advice, assist with the application process, and help you navigate the complexities of these options.

**Tips for accelerating mortgage payments and saving on interest**

Accelerating mortgage payments and saving on interest can help you pay off your mortgage faster and reduce the overall cost of your loan. Here are some tips to consider:

1. Make Bi-Weekly Payments: Instead of paying your mortgage once a month, consider making bi-weekly payments. By doing this, you'll make 26 half-payments in a year, which is equivalent to 13 full payments. This strategy can help you pay off your mortgage earlier and save on interest over the life of the loan.

2. Round Up Your Payments: Another simple strategy is to round up your mortgage payments. For example, if your monthly payment is $1,200, consider paying $1,300 or even $1,500. The extra amount will go towards the principal balance, reducing the overall interest paid and shortening the loan term.

3. Make Extra Principal Payments: Whenever you have some extra money, consider making additional payments towards the principal balance of your mortgage. This can help you pay off the loan faster and save on interest. Even small additional payments can make a significant difference over time.

4. Refinance to a Shorter Term: If your financial situation allows, consider refinancing your mortgage to a shorter term, such as from a 30-year to a 15-year loan. While your monthly payments may increase, you'll pay off the loan faster and save a substantial amount on interest.

5. Avoid Adjustable Rate Mortgages (ARMs): If you have an adjustable rate mortgage, consider refinancing to a fixed-rate mortgage. Fixed-rate mortgages provide stability by locking in your interest rate, protecting you from potential rate increases in the future.

6. Avoid Private Mortgage Insurance (PMI): If you have a conventional loan and are paying for private mortgage insurance, try to reach the point where you have at least 20% equity in your home. Once you reach this point, you can request to have the PMI removed, which will lower your monthly payment and save you money over time.

7. Consider Mortgage Recasting: Mortgage recasting allows you to make a lump sum payment towards the principal balance of your mortgage and have your monthly payments recalculated based on the new reduced balance. This can lower your monthly payments without the need to refinance.

8. Shop Around for Lower Interest Rates: Keep an eye on interest rates and consider refinancing if you can secure a lower rate. Lower

interest rates can significantly reduce your monthly payment and save you money on interest over the life of the loan.

Remember to consult with your lender or a mortgage professional to understand the specific terms and conditions of your mortgage, as well as any prepayment penalties that may apply. They can provide personalized advice based on your financial situation and help you determine the best strategies to accelerate your mortgage payments and save on interest.

## 11.   Conclusion

**Recap of key strategies for saving money on a home mortgage**

Here's a recap of the key strategies for saving money on a home mortgage:

1. Make bi-weekly payments or round up your payments to accelerate the repayment process and save on interest.

2. Make extra principal payments whenever possible to reduce the overall loan balance and shorten the loan term.

3. Consider refinancing to a shorter term mortgage, such as from a 30-year to a 15-year loan, to pay off the mortgage faster and save on interest.

4. Avoid adjustable rate mortgages (ARMs) and opt for fixed-rate mortgages to avoid potential interest rate increases in the future.

5. Reach at least 20% equity in your home to eliminate the need for private mortgage insurance (PMI) and reduce your monthly payment.

6. Explore mortgage recasting, which allows you to make a lump sum payment towards the principal balance and have your monthly payments recalculated based on the reduced balance.

7. Stay updated on interest rates and consider refinancing if you can secure a lower rate, as it can significantly reduce your monthly payment and save you money on interest.

Remember to consult with your lender or a mortgage professional to get personalized advice based on your specific situation and mortgage terms. They can provide guidance tailored to your needs and help you make informed decisions.

**Encouragement and motivation for taking control of your mortgage journey**

Taking control of your mortgage journey is a significant step towards financial empowerment and achieving your long-term goals. Here's some encouragement and motivation to inspire you:

1. Financial Freedom: By actively managing your mortgage, you are taking charge of your financial future. Imagine the peace of mind and freedom that comes with owning your home outright or being mortgage-free sooner than expected.

2. Building Equity: Every payment you make towards your mortgage builds equity in your home. This means you are gradually increasing your ownership stake and building wealth over time. Keep envisioning the satisfaction of knowing you're building a valuable asset.

3. Saving Money: By implementing strategies to save money on your mortgage, such as making extra payments or refinancing, you can potentially save thousands of dollars in interest payments. Imagine what you could do with that extra money – invest, save for retirement, or even treat yourself to something special.

4. Achieving Goals: Taking control of your mortgage journey puts you on the path to achieving your other financial goals. Whether it's starting a business, saving for your children's education, or planning for retirement, the savings and financial stability gained from managing your mortgage can help you make progress towards those aspirations.

5. Empowerment: Being proactive and informed about your mortgage gives you a sense of empowerment and control over your financial life. It shows that you are committed to making smart decisions and taking responsibility for your financial well-being.

Remember, the journey to mortgage success may not always be easy, but stay focused on the end goal and the positive impact it will have on your life. You have the power to shape your financial future, and by taking control of your mortgage, you are taking a significant step towards a brighter and more secure financial future. Keep going, and don't hesitate to seek guidance from professionals along the way. You've got this!

Dear Readers,

I hope this letter finds you well. I wanted to take a moment to express my sincerest appreciation for your support in reading my book, "Mortgage Mastery: The Ultimate Guide to Saving Money on Your Home Mortgage." It is an honor to have you as my readers, and I am truly grateful for the opportunity to share my knowledge and insights with you.

Writing this book has been a labor of love, with the goal of empowering homeowners like you to make informed decisions and save money on your home mortgages. It is my hope that the strategies and tips shared within these pages have provided you with valuable guidance and a deeper understanding of the mortgage process.

As an author, I value your feedback immensely. Your honest reviews play a crucial role in not only helping me improve as a writer but also in guiding other potential readers towards this book. Your thoughts and opinions have the power to influence others and encourage them to take control of their mortgage journey.

I kindly request a few minutes of your time to leave an honest review on your preferred platform or website. Whether you choose to share your thoughts on the practical tips, the clarity of the content, or how the book has positively impacted your financial situation, every review is invaluable. Your words have the potential to reach and assist countless homeowners in their quest to save money on their mortgages.

Once again, I want to express my deepest gratitude for your support. Your readership and engagement mean the world to me, and I am honored to be a part of your journey towards financial freedom. Thank you for choosing "Mortgage Mastery" and for allowing me to be your guide in navigating the complex world of home mortgages.

Wishing you continued success in your homeownership journey, and I look forward to sharing more valuable insights with you in the future.

Warmest regards,

Mark Livingston